I0419433

Steven Lloyd

Bleed With Me

BLEED WITH ME

Copyright © 2016 by Steven Lloyd

This book is a work of nonfiction. All rights reserved. No part of this book may be used or reproduced in any manner whatsoever without written permission (except in the case of brief quotations embodied in critical articles and reviews).

ISBN-10: 1539366847
ISBN-13: 978-1539366843

Cover Art and Design by Zach McCain

Book Design by César Puch

Printed in the United States of America

PRAISE FOR STEVEN LLOYD

"Naked Snake Press published When Darkness Falls by Steven Lloyd, about an elderly man who tells his grandson a frightening story about his youth—only some of which is true. The truth is much more horrifying."

—Ellen Datlow

"Steven Lloyd's *When Darkness Falls* showcases an original take on the idea of serial killing and supernatural revenge. Lloyd crafts some creepy mojo from the get-go and never lets up."

—Bryan Smith, author of *House of Blood* and *Deathbringer*

"Creepy stuff! A wild ride indeed...call me a big fan, 'cause I look forward to reading this guy for years to come...

—James Newman (*Midnight Rain, Holy Rollers*)
(For "When Darkness Fall")

"A genuinely creepy trip to the dark side. Read it at night with the lights down low, and feel the chill."

—Bill Crider, author of *Keepers of The Beast*.
(For "When Darkness Fall")

"The best horror stories are those that rip out human emotions and place them under a microscrope for closer inspection. In 'The Wooden Box,' Steven Lloyd takes a hard look at love and death without relying on the supernatural to create a sense of foreboding and dread. Instead, the ghosts in this story are the memories of better days as a husband gives one final gift to his dying wife. At times both touching and disturbing, 'The Wooden Box' is a gripping story that builds to an unsettling conclusion."

—Jason Brannon

"Fascinating!"

—T.M. Wright, author of *The Strange Seed*, *Blue Canoe*, and *The House on Orchid Street* (For "The Wooden Box")

"'The Wooden Box' is as excruciating as it is uplifting. It's a simple parable, but it packs a strong punch."

—The Horror Drive-In

"'The Wooden Box' is powerful, tough, and tender. Read it and see what I mean."

—Bill Crider

"A beautiful story."

—Kealan Patrick Burke (For "The Wooden Box")

"An incredible Writer."

—Ronald Kelly
(For "The Wooden Box")

"Full of well developed characters, sharp twists and turns, and a compelling story, I think that if you dig horror, you'll dig this book. Don't pass it up."

—Eric S. Brown

For Martha Damico

"Writing is the hardest work in the world. I have been a bricklayer and a truck driver, and I tell you—as if you haven't been told a million times already—that writing is harder. Lonelier. And nobler and more enriching. The trick is not becoming a writer. The trick is staying a writer. Get a day job, make your money from that, and write to please yourself."

—Harlan Ellison

Foreword

What makes a writer a great writer?

Is it financial success? If that is the case, Stephanie Meyer, E.L. James, and James Patterson Incorporated are the best authors since Shakespeare. Some people buy into that mindset, but I am not one of them. When you follow logic of that sort, Taco Bell is among the world's best food.

Critical acclaim? Yeah, that certainly helps, but there's the old adage about the only good critic being a dead one. You never know which ones are sincere, or whether the review has been bought and paid for. We've all heard rumors of that sort of thing going on.

How about acceptance and praise from fellow professionals? That carries greater weight for many, and it's understandable. But I think there is one more important factor in determining a great writer from a bad one, or even a good one.

The ultimate judge is *you*. Me. Anyone who picks up a piece of fiction, and is transformed to another place. Whose life is changed, maybe temporarily, or sometimes even permanently.

When a writer takes us by the hands and knocks our socks right the hell off.

Which brings me to Steven Lloyd.

Prior to 2014 I knew of Steven Lloyd's work as a publisher. He founded Croatoan Press in 2008, and while the company didn't last as long as many hoped it would, Lloyd published some nice books, and unlike others, I don't believe that he left any animosity in wake. The man had bigger fish to fry, and he moved on.

Some years passed, and I was going through my own forms of Hell. At a low point in my life, Steven Lloyd sent me a hand bound manuscript of a story called *The Wooden Box*. I filed it in an ever-expanding mass of fiction to be read that typically puts The Blob to shame. I didn't leave it there for long. I picked up *The Wooden Box* a week or two after receiving it and I began to read.

I knew immediately that I was in the hands of a great writer.

The Wooden Box is a achingly sad story. Almost unbearable, even. But Lloyd seemed to know that the reader wants more than despair from a work of fiction. In a very few pages he takes us into the depths of loss and grief, but the real gift of the story is the grace in which he takes his tale. That and the care Lloyd puts into every sentence.

Yeah, regardless of whatever else Steven Lloyd may write, and whether or not his work equals *The Wooden Box*, the man is a great writer. Even if he never published another word in his life.

But, thankfully, he has published more. More short fiction resides in an excellent collection called Strange Roads. And with more fiction on the way, hopefully including a novel.

His work as a short story writer has drawn acclaim from unimpeachable sources. Lloyd has done editorial work. He has been a journalist. The guy has been around.

And now Steven Lloyd shares some of his experience and hard sense in the pages of this book. Part confessional, part instructional, Mr. Lloyd shares some of the darkness from his past, and reveals how it has helped him as a writer. He details the pitfalls he and many, many, other aspiring writers fall into. He may tell you some stuff you won't want to hear, but I urge you to at least listen and take heed. It's a hard, strange road out there on the path to publication, and he's here to help you out a little along the way. The real work will be yours, as will the success or failure you will achieve. He's merely here to provide you with some practical advice.

Along with the advice, Lloyd demonstrates how clear, clean, effective prose can be delivered with excerpts from his own writing.

If all that ain't enough, Steven Lloyd has kindly added the complete text of *The Wooden Box* to this chest of wonders and horrors. Go on, don't be afraid. Turn the page, and bleed with him.

—Mark Sieber
September 2016

Introduction

Before I knew Steven Lloyd as a friend, he was a complete and total stranger. This isn't surprising; most friendships start in such a way.

Before I knew him as a writer, I knew him as an editor and publisher. Now, this *was* surprising. *Very* surprising. Generally, most editors and publishers are content with wearing those hats and those alone. There are exceptions, though. Richard Chizmar of Cemetery Dance and David Wilson of Crossroad Press are a couple of examples. And, like them, Steven is a damn good writer. He's been around. He's paid his share of dues...and then some.

The first time I came across his name was when I went on Robert McCammon's discussion forum in the summer of 2006 and formally announced that I would be returning to the horror genre after a self-imposed exile of ten years. I was hesitant and uncertain– actually scared shitless, is putting it lightly – because starting all over again seemed like a daunting and impossible task. Later that evening, I went back to the forum and was encouraged by the comments and support my announcement had conjured. And there was one in particular from some guy named Steven Lloyd that I remember word-for-word. He said *"Wow! I come home from work and find that the great Ron Kelly is in the house! How cool is that?"* Now, you can imagine how I felt, reading that. It was an ego boost of Red Bull six-pack proportions... especially for someone who hadn't had his ego boosted for nearly a decade.

Shortly after that, we quickly became good friends and fellow peers in the horror genre. He was an editor for Nocturne Press at the time and wanted to publish a limited hardcover of *Undertaker's Moon* (*Moon of the Werewolf* to you old-time Zebra readers out there) with a phenomenal cover by an artist by the name of Alex McVey. During that time, I made new friends in the horror circle: folks like Alex, James Newman, Zach McCain, Donn Gash, Jason Brannon, and César Puch. Unfortunately, before *UM* could be published, Nocturne went out of business. After that Steven launched his own publishing house, Croatoan Publishing, and released two beautiful books; Newman's *People Are Strange* and a slick reprint of my post-apocalyptic horror novella, *Flesh-Welder*. The potential for Croatoan was monumental, but, like many small press endeavors, the financial stability was not. Sadly, CP went the way of the dodo bird and the 20-cent comic book, but not before Steven put a copy of *Flesh-Welder* in every goody-bag at the 2007 World Horror Convention.

And there were other acts of professionalism and utter kindness that Steven blessed me with around that time of transition back into the writing world; ones I've kept to myself... until now. Upon finding out that I couldn't afford a trip to Hypericon in 2007, Steven graciously footed the bill, paying for my food and hotel room for the weekend. I can never express my gratitude for that gesture…it was far beyond the call of duty and I appreciate it deeply to this day.

After Croatoan's demise, Steven sort of faded out of the picture for a while. Then he sent me a couple of short stories to read… stories written by *him*. I must admit, for a moment I thought to myself, "Oh no… not one of *those* guys!" But then I read them and was genuinely impressed. His work was a little rough around the edges, but held tremendous potential. I voluntarily edited some of his work and he began submitting them. Then his writing career just sort of took off, like a bare-assed cat in a bucket of turpentine. Soon, I found a copy of *The Wooden Box* in my hands and I knew he was destined for literary greatness.

So, let's talk about what you hold in *your* hands. This small, but potent publication called *Bleed With Me*. Should you take Steven Lloyd's words at face value? Should you heed his warnings and follow his advice concerning the trappings and mechanics of, not only the horror genre, but *any* genre of the literary spectrum?

My answer? A resounding *yes!* Unlike other instructional books on the writing business, you have a rare three-for-one here, folks. An experienced and accomplished writer, publisher, *and* editor, all rolled into one. If anyone can instruct you, without a shred of pretentious bullshit whatsoever, on the wonders and woes of the writing business, it is this man.

As well as advice, he has presented examples of his own prose, including a special treat… *The Wooden Box*, in its entirety. Remember, Steven is no stranger to the rough and rocky roads you are traveling on the way to publication. He's been where you have been, where you are now, and where you will be one year… five years… ten years from now. With his help, you'll find your road easier to navigate, with less rocks and potholes than you are experiencing right now.

And, more than likely, when you finally accomplish your writing goals and reach the end of that road, he'll be there with a big shit-eating grin on his face, waiting for you.

—Ronald Kelly
Brush Creek, Tennessee
September 2016

Bleed With Me

Chapter One

Dark Days

My uncle said that my father's sons are cursed. I don't know about all that. Does make one wonder.

I once walked five miles home from school in the winter. The teacher wouldn't call on me. I knew the answers. I went so unnoticed I slipped out into the hall, collected my jacket hanging on the coatrack and headed home.

*

By the time I reached the halfway point, I couldn't feel my fingers and toes. Luckily a pickup truck pulled off onto the shoulder of the freeway ahead of me. An old man got out. I still remember his words. "You lost your mind, boy?"

I was five.

Shit happens.

*

I'm a nobody. I travel the literary landscape without brand or name. Yet people whisper my name behind closed doors, and in dark places. I've done well over the years with my writing. I took risks. Developed close, personal relationships with people in the industry. I hold them close to my heart to this day. That's why I've decided to write this short book. To give you the advice I wish I'd had in the beginning. There would've been less mess. Not saying you, new writer, won't make mistakes because you will. We all do. But this will give you a head start. Let no one tell you that you can't become a published writer. Ever.

*

I wasn't born a writer. None of us are. Perhaps it stalked me my whole life. Who knows? But once it grabbed me, that was it. I was hooked. My mind grew that third eye writers talk of and off I went, soaring into the darkest of places. Because, you know, that's what writers do. We take you to places you otherwise wouldn't go, or see.

*

It takes more than imagination. It takes more than thinking about it. It takes talent and practice and hunger. This hunger is never sated. No how-to book on writing ever helped me more than the writers who grace my bookshelves. Want to know how to write well? Read everything. Don't limit yourself to one genre. Expand your reading. I did. So should you.

I often hear the question: "Can people be taught how to write?" Yes.

*

When I started writing at the age of fifteen, I couldn't tell a verb from an adverb. I couldn't tell you anything about conjunctions. Teachers found it almost impossible to teach me. I was so hyperactive I couldn't learn anything.

*

When I was a sophomore in high school, my English instructor wanted us to write a horror story for the month of October. What a drag, right? I hated writing anything. Only because I was forced, I wrote a story called *Killing Vengeance*, a bloody story about a boy who goes after a group of men for killing his family. Two weeks later I read this little story in front of the class. I have horrible stage fright. It takes a special kind of voice to pull this off. I, unfortunately, don't have the talent for public readings. More interested in how I looked and sounded, I didn't hear the hush fall over the class. You could've heard a mouse fart. I looked up from my paper. In that moment I was calculating how long I'd be suspended from school. I'd written something bloody and dreadful. People died in my story. This, I assured myself, was not going to go unpunished. My parents would be called—bet on that one, and I'd be grounded until my hair either fell out or turned gray. When the bell rang I made for the door. Fast. The teacher, a small woman of about fifty, took hold of me and sat me down. When the class emptied, she said, (I'll never forget her words) 'You have a great talent, Steven. Don't ever stop.' If only I could tell her what I've accomplished as a writer. Thinking about it now, that lovable old lady probably kept those assignments coming because she saw my potential. And, yes, I fell in love with reading. How can you write and not read? This is a must!

*

Let's get personal before we embark on this crazy-ass journey, shall we? I owe you that much. We're going to talk about things I've kept hidden. Things about me, things about my family. Stuff with which paved the way for my own writing. Life can slip in and make its own road for you. This is the road that led me to where I am today.

*

By the time I turned seventeen, I was arrested and thrown out of school for selling grass and carrying a concealed weapon. My father found himself yet again in court with one of his kids. I wound up in Coordinated Youth, a program for troubled kids. Hal, an older teacher, saw something in me I didn't. Hope. Hal took me under his wing. Folks, books and writing saved my life. I read and wrote voraciously. Little by little I began to learn what I needed to know about stringing words together. This took a long time. Nothing happens overnight, new writer. I had to work for it. So will you.

Chapter Two

The Blood That Binds

My brother John has spent much of his life behind bars—seven minimum security prisons and eight maximum, to be exact.

Correctional facilities once hosted picnics for their inmates and their families. This was the norm growing up in the '70s and '80s for my family. Times have changed, though and the practice of picnics on the yard was suspended indefinitely due to constant contraband being smuggled in by family members. I grew up seeing mine through the gears of the correctional machine.

In our youth, my younger brother, Christopher and I walked the halls of murderer's rapists and pedophiles. The dregs of society.

On one visit with my brother, I shook hands with a man who had murdered four family members with an ax. Course I didn't know this until later in life. It was this same man who collected myself and my brother when we ventured too far away from the picnic area and found ourselves in the restricted area—a basketball court of all places. Sirens blared. Armed guards rushed the catwalks of the giant walls. Jimmy, this same man who years before had brutally murdered members of his family, rushed to our rescue, collected us like lost sheep, and herded us back to the safe zone.

A few years later John was doing a stretch for DUI at Vienna Correctional Center in Illinois. This is where I met serial killer William George Heirens. Heirens' third and final victim, six-year-old Suzanne Degnan, met her fate in a basement apartment laundry room four decades earlier. Heirens distributed portions of the child's body throughout the city, leaving a nation stunned. I sat four feet from this beast in the early '80s. I saw his face, his hands with which worked the blade so long ago. I looked into his eyes. Cold. Though we never communicated, his eyes spoke volumes.

Heirens' two previous victims, Josephine Ross and Frances Brown, were found stabbed to death in their apartments. On the scene police noted the inscription on the wall written in lipstick, *For heaven's sake catch me before I kill more I cannot control myself,* thus giving him the nickname The Lipstick Killer. Heirens was the oldest living serial killer incarcerated until his death on March 5, 2012, at the age of 83.

Heirens would not be my last encounter with true evil.

*

A few months later we made the pilgrimage to *Dwight Correctional Center* outside Chicago to see my older sister, who was doing 20 years to life for the murder of an elderly woman by the name of Martha Damico.

On a cold February morning in 1973, my sister, Cynthia Barnes, entered the home of 51-year-old Martha Damico. Damico had told my sister that her daughter had left for school early that morning. Cynthia asked to use the phone. Confined to a wheelchair, Martha let my sister inside to use the phone, which would prove fatal.

The assault began once the door closed. My sister's first attempt was to strangle Martha Damico with a pair of pantyhose. When the pantyhose ripped she tore the phone cord from the wall to strangle Damico. Still unsure if she'd done the job, my sister found a meat fork, which she used to stab Martha Damico repeatedly. After the deed she stole fourteen dollars and some cosmetics, purchased a pair of jeans at a local outlet and then left town. She was quickly apprehended in Chicago and plead guilty to the slaying. She was seventeen. During the trial my father called for the death penalty. In the mid-90s she was paroled after a twenty-year sentence.

I filed all this away thirty plus years ago. You too will file things away to use in your own writing one day, whether it be for fiction or non-fiction.

Chapter Three

Too Much Self-doubt
Can be a Foundation for Failure

Writers are a strange bunch. Ask my wife. I like simple. Change is never good for me. At night I draw the blinds and lock the doors—sometimes rechecking them many times before I'm content. I live my existence as if I have no neighbors. I'm familiar with more people on the Internet than who lives next door to me. Fixed in my ways. Nothing, as far as I know, will ever change this. All this drives my wife crazy. But she deals with my insanities the only way she knows how—by ignoring it.

My father introduced me to black and white horror films from *his* era. From there I graduated to more modern films such as Jason Voorhees, Michael Myers, and Leatherface. But I see myself moving away from horror little by little. Though I'll still have that dark quality in my writing, I find ghosts and goblins a thing of the past—at least for me. We live real life horror every waking hour of our lives. We see it on the news. Our whole lives are consumed with it.

Even when my writing was toilet stink—and it was because I reread my earlier work—my father pushed me forward. Told me

I could accomplish anything through persistence and dedication. And here I am today at forty-three hitting the keys and eager to build an audience.

All writers have self-doubt. It happens. Six years running, I attended Hypericon Convention in Nashville, TN. James Newman, a promising up and comer, had a terrible bout with self-doubt after the release of his novel *Midnight Rain*. This wasn't a small press release, folks. Dorchester Publishing out of New York accepted Midnight Rain and ran with it. If you haven't read his work, correct this immediately. James is a powerhouse that should never be taken lightly. Course I couldn't convince him that 'Rain' was *not* a fluke. He must have realized this later because he has now gone on to write some wonderful stuff.

I *do* worry about not reaching that level with my next project. See? There's that dreaded self-doubt seeping in. Don't let it get to you. Fight through it. Stave off the wolves. Move forward.

Most of the best books on writing are short and to the point. These are things that have helped me through the years. You may find something useful here too.

Like the title of this book reads, bleed with me, baby, and put them boots on cause we're goin' wadin'.

Chapter Four
The Truth

Mainstream publishing is a cluster-fuck. I've spent twenty-five years behind the keyboard in hopes of becoming a professional writer who's paid a living.

I'm a closet procrastinator. Few people know this about me. Lack of faith and procrastinating can snuff the fire. I have no set rituals, though I do enjoy writing outdoors. Writing in cold blood isn't for me. Jack London once said, *"You can't wait for inspiration. You have to go after it with a club."* Constant readers are not stupid. They know when the writing is on mark, or if the author is rushing or writing without fire. I don't always write every day, but I do read every day. I find reading sparks my muse more than anything. Reading is a must.

*

In 2012 I wrote and self-published a fiction piece titled *The Wooden Box*. The story reached critical acclaim and put me on the literary map. I finally had something good. *The Wooden Box* remains a fan favorite in the small press to this day. The reality of it all hit me. Before I embarked on the self-publishing train, I submitted the story to the large magazines. At least one of these giants would publish this story, right? Nope. *The Wooden Box* found no home and was rejected by all the major magazines. This was a turning point in my career as a writer. The truth is that major publishers don't give a shit how good your novel or story is, hence the title of this article. It's not about how long you've been in the business. It's about whom you know. It's about popular brand and name. I know a writer who writes children stories for a major New York publisher. Sounds cool, huh? Said writer finishes the story and the publisher slaps a celebrity's name on the cover to sell copies. Not cool.

CHAPTER FIVE

The Long Sleep

In 2001, I was searching for myself. I hadn't written anything in ten years, and one day my *then* girlfriend bought me a computer. Voices once silent now began to talk. The stories I wanted to tell came easily. My first acceptance came in '05 when Naked Snake Press released my short story *When Darkness Falls* as a standalone chapbook. The next year brought good news when Ellen Datlow mentioned the story in her Summation within "The Year's Best Fantasy and Horror" 2006. I was blown away, and I made sure to call friends and family to let them know. For me, it was just as good as having my story published in the book. I have it on my shelf today. And in 2014 my short story collection *Strange Roads* found itself on the *recommended list* for the Bram Stoker Award. Never stop dreaming.

Chapter Six

Throw Fame and Riches to the Wind

Don't worry about accolades and money and fame. Write the stories you want and send them out. If you're in it for money and fame, you need to pack your bags and move on, because it rarely happens. Publishers don't take risks. You have a stadium of sixty thousand writers waiting for their shot, and only five or six will make a career of it.

*

Aspiring writers have the misconception they're going to be an overnight sensation. Seasoned writers wonder if their day will ever come. Some on both sides have quit writing altogether, giving up the game. New York publishers refer to books as "units," and have for many, many years. This depresses me on so many levels. After "Fifty Shades of Gray" and pop star Kanye West's "Thank You and You're Welcome," I realized publishing had become a world of brands and names. I came to the conclusion I was never going to make a living at the writing gig.

And you know what, I could write free of stress and without heartache.

CHAPTER SEVEN

How to Contact Your Favorite Author for a Blurb

THIS CAN BE TRICKY. TRUST ME. I'VE DONE IT. THIS IS SOMETHING you ease into. Never beat your favorite author over the head with your book. Think about it as going on your first date. You'd never ask your date for oral sex at dinner, now would you? Of course not. No one ever succeeded at anything by being rude. Tell them how much their writing impacted your life. Writers like to hear this stuff. It's the go-juice that keeps on giving. And always use the word *potential*. For example, "Would you mind reading my book for a *potential* blurb?" This gives them an exit if they accept to read it and hate it. Most writers worth their salt are not in the game to crush aspiring writers. If you don't receive a reply, drop it. Don't send a follow up email. Let it go. Lesson learned. If you do hear back, send the book with a thank you. During this time be patient and move on with your day. The ball is in their court. Don't nag. This will force your favorite author into a corner. Know what happens when you corner a boar? Okay. Don't do it.

*

No other writer has inspired me more than award winning author Bill Crider. I didn't know Bill Crider then; I knew his dark passenger *Jack MacLane*. Jack took me to places I *wanted* to go. His writing opened my mind to what I wanted to be in life: A writer of stories. I've read great books since, but nothing captivated my nineteen-year-old imagination as much as *Rest in Peace*, Bill's 1990 Zebra release. The book gave me the wings I needed to take flight. And then one day he was gone. He just up and vanished. Or so I thought. In 2005 I learned that Bill had not vanished, but continued to write under his real name. In that same year my short story *When Darkness Falls* found a home at Naked Snake Press. While waiting on the final proofs, I found Bill's website and thought *what if...*

Contacting this larger-than-life writer for a blurb terrified me. My hands trembled at the keyboard. The man who had changed my life with just one book was on the other side of that "send" icon. I walked outside to smoke, my mind racing, and my hands still trembling at the thought of clicking *send*. I rushed back to the computer and sent the email. A week went by. Two weeks. On the third week Bill replied with an enthusiastic yes! I sent off the story immediately. This is what I got back:

"A genuinely creepy trip to the dark side. Read it at night with the lights down low, and feel the chill."

In 2012 he blessed me yet again with a blurb for my short story *The Wooden Box*.

CHAPTER EIGHT

To Review or Not to Review

A WRITER WHO ARGUES WITH A REVIEWER NEEDS TO THROW A rope over their shoulder and pull their head out of their ass. Never argue with a reviewer. I don't care if they're wrong. Don't sweat it. Never have family review your book. This cannot happen. Amazon removes reviews if they think the reviewer is related. And it makes you look amateur. Never trade reviews with another writer. Remember, you want to be respected in the business. Doing a favor in the long run will hurt your credibility. Once that's gone, it's gone. I released *Strange Roads* two years ago. Know how many reviews I have? Six. Not many, huh? But they're six honest reviews. And, before you ask, three star reviews are good.

*

Never make the Anne Rice mistake. What? What do you mean? About eleven or twelve years ago, Anne Rice verbally attacked reviewers on Amazon for giving honest feedback after reading her new release. This went on for several days. Never have I seen such unprofessionalism by a single author. Much respect was lost. Don't repeat it. Your job is to write. I once blocked a friend on Facebook because he asked his fans (I use the word *fans* loosely) to attack a reviewer for leaving a two-star review.

Chapter Nine
Social Media

Social Media is a great thing, isn't it? Sure it is. This is a place a writer can spread his or her wings and promote endlessly. Yet there are problems a writer can face. But Steve, how can this be a problem? Getting to that. New writers hit Facebook daily looking to sell their books. No problem. We've all done it. Even seasoned writers do it. To a point. Once someone has accepted your friend request, never send them a "like my page" until you get acquainted. Even then you need to ask permission. Unless you're a close friend, this usually gets you blocked. Well, unless you're Clive Barker, Stephen King or any other major star in the publishing world. Yeah, I know, double standard sucks.

*

Most new writers make the mistake of adding "Author John Doe/Jane Doe" at the top of their Facebook page. Don't do this. Why? No one cares who you are. And most established writers laugh at this sort of thing, and have no problem doing so publicly.

Award Winning author Tim Waggoner said it best:

Public Service Announcement: New writers, when someone posts on FB asking what authors people recommend, Don't. Name. Your. Fucking. Self. Ever. It's a total dick-noob move and makes you look like a dumbass.

I don't know Tim other than his work, but the quote above must be taught to aspiring writers before hitting Facebook. Out of respect I asked Tim if I could use the quote above. If in doubt always ask. You can visit Tim Waggoner here:

http://timwaggoner.com/index.htm

Moving on.

*

Self-publishing companies swim the same waters on Facebook as you do. I can't tell you how many times I've watched new writers fall head over heels in love with their offers of success. I'll tell you now there's little success here. Most times they take your money and leave you out in the cold, promising you a life of promotion and brick and mortar book sales. What they won't tell you is that unless they have a return policy, bookstores won't take the title. First thing you need to ask is if they have a return policy with bookstores. If not, don't do it. As I said, they swim in the same waters you do, so keep your wits. Never be taken in by false dreams.

Chapter Ten

The Literary Boom
Heard Around the World

Most new writers won't know this, so it's imperative if not our duty as established writers, to teach those coming into the field what occurred in the mid-90s. Reason being: it can happen again. The fallout still remains one of the most devastating and catastrophic attacks on the literary world to ever take place.

*

Giant publishing firms moved in and swallowed up all the little publishing houses. Horror wouldn't see the light of day until the mid-2000s. As they say: those who forget the past are doomed to repeat it.

*

Writer and friend, Ronald Kelly made his mark with his first book *Hindsight*. Five or six successful books followed. *Fear* still remains one of my all-time favorite books. His agent called one day asking if he could write anything other than horror. Ron had written horror from the beginning. Ron told him no. Ron's career ended that day. Hundreds if not thousands of other writers endured the same fate. Writers scrambled to find homes for their work. Some did, others did not. Ronald chose to leave the publishing world and return to factory work. He wrote nothing for twelve years. Ronald returned to the publishing industry with a vengeance in 2005 with new work and a fresh start. He has gone on to write several new books, along with bringing back some oldies.

Chapter Eleven

Strange Roads
and How It Happened

In 2013, I felt the need to gather some of my favorite stories and put them in one collection. All the stories except two were traditionally published in one magazine or another. I wanted to be remembered. So will you. I went the self-publishing route with Strange Roads because I didn't think a publisher would work with a bunch of reprints from a guy who didn't have a fairly big name. This is the part where I tell you how to do this the correct way. You're going to spend money if you want to put out your book. These are the steps I took. Take everything I say with a grain of salt. What worked for me may not work for you.

1. Never use the self-publishing website to do the work for you. Go out and find people in the small press who take pride in their work. Ask around.

2. Find a great artist for your book cover. The cover of your book means everything. It will be the first thing people see. Most artists charge a flat fee upfront between $200 to $500.

3. Choose an interior book designer. He/she will make the inside text rock! Find a good one. Most charge about $2 or $3 dollars per page. This is also paid upfront.

4. Choose an editor worth his/her salt. This is tricky. Unfortunately, we have people who prey on the aspiring. Never, ever send your book out unedited. You've got one shot in this business to make a splash, don't fuck it up. You can do a million things right and do one thing wrong, and that's what you'll be remembered for. Don't be that person.

5. I paid out about $800 for Strange Roads to a group of friends I trusted to help me look my best. Then I uploaded all my files. I used Createspace to publish Strange Roads. This cost me $0. I didn't need their team because I had my own. Even then I found some errors in the book that were missed once it came out. Do the best you can. Pony up the money if you want to look good.

Chapter Twelve

The Trash We Keep in the Box

NOT LONG AGO I COMMITTED THE CARDINAL SIN: I TRASHED ALL my old work from my early days. Several thousand stories met the flame. Hand written, typed, it didn't matter, the fire has no prejudice. Course these were stories I wrote between my teen years into my early twenties. One collection I kept and sent off to a friend because she was bored and wanted something funny to read. So, like a good friend should, I indulged her. Told her to pop some popcorn and lay back and laugh. Did she? Have no clue. Sometimes you've got to shake yourself loose of the old shit. Things you know you're never going to use. And, you know, it cleans out the brain cells.

Chapter Thirteen

Dialog

THE BEST WAY TO LEARN DIALOG IS TO GET OUT MORE. LISTEN TO others talk. Go to the mall. Find a bench and open your ears. Listen to our fellow humans talk. Read Joe R. Lansdale and Elmore Leonard, two of the finest dialog writers. Let me give you some real life dialog I've incorporated into my own work.

*

Normally my commute to work takes about fifteen minutes. No biggie. On a warm summer morning last year, we got hit with fog so thick it took me forty-five minutes. Arriving, I tucked my lunch away and headed outside to smoke before my shift started. Orvid, one of my best friends, told me he'd be right out to join me. He nicknamed me the iron lung. Yeah, I smoke a lot. Not something you want to brag about. Anyhow, I *heard* the door open. I couldn't see shit. It reminded me of Stephen King's *The Mist*. Then we collided. The impact nearly sent us to the ground. Now, this is what was said. Always remember an exchange of good dialog.

"Goddamn," Orvid said.

"You okay?"

"Yeah, lost my fuckin' cigarette. Got one?"

"Here," I said.

"Goddamn, can't see you white fuckers in the fog, and you can't see us black mother fuckers in the dark."

"That's some racist shit, man."

"True that."

*

Below is from my short story *Black Mountain*.

Floyd Carlson awoke as the storm battered the cabin. The wind whistled and slapped the two-story structure. He slipped out of bed and pulled on his clothes and gun belt, slipped the twin colts out of their holsters to check their loads, and then he slipped them back into their holsters. He walked over to the window. From there he saw the barn. Through the wind he heard Popcorn. Kim, his wife, slept on her side. He shook her. Her eyes fluttered open.

"What's wrong?" Her voice groggy with sleep, she rolled over. "Floyd?"

"We need to get downstairs. I'll get the boy."

"Is it the storm?"

"Yes."

"Okay," Kim said and got up. She was about to wrap herself in her robe, but Floyd stopped her.

"Clothes," Floyd said. "Just in case. Never heard wind like this." Floyd left the room and walked down the hall to his son's room. He was awake and staring out the window. The boy looked over his shoulder. "Wind woke me, Papa."

"I see."

"We going downstairs?"

"Until the storm passes. What you lookin' at?"

"Them."

Floyd put a hand on the colt's grip and walked over and looked out the window. The only thing he could see was snow and trees. "Them who, boy?"

"Ones I see every night?"

"See what, boy? Nothin' out there but trees and snow and wind."

Russell pointed and said, "They stay behind the trees mostly."

His father cupped his hands against the cold pane of glass. "Damn if I can see anything. We got to get downstairs." Floyd found Russell's clothes draped over the chair back in the corner of the room. "Put these on and hurry. None of us need to be up here right now." Russell dressed and followed his father downstairs. Kim sat in her reading chair.

"Popcorn's havin' a fit," Kim said.

Floyd pulled on his coat. "I know. Heading out now."

"I can help, Papa," said Russell. "Can I come?"

"Next time."

Kim got up and went about making coffee. "Don't be long. Get him taken care of and get back here. Knew better to go to sleep. Thank God we got up when you did."

"It is."

And then he opened the door and was gone.

Floyd shouldered open the barn door and stepped inside. Birds scattered, escaping the onrush of wind then settled back in the rafters as he forced the door closed. The owl remained motionless and vigilant, and sidestepped to get a better look at who walked inside.

Popcorn, a mustang of seven years, snorted and stomped the hay-strewn floor of his stall. He circled the thing half a dozen times, skittish and troubled. Then he quieted, settling near the back of the stall.

Floyd had bought him as a foal on the day of his son's birth. Little Russell enjoyed riding almost as much as he did. Russell, now seven, cared for Popcorn daily, but the snowstorm had moved in and put a stop to that.

"What's got into you, boy?" Popcorn stamped the floor and snorted and circled the stall one time. "Storms come and go. You feel it too, don't you? Something around here I should know about?" Floyd chuckled as if the horse might tell him a story. He listened to cracking limbs and howls not matching the wind at all. It grew louder and closer.

"Settle down, boy," Floyd said. "It'll pass." He found his black leather chest up against a stall gate and opened it. He unfolded the wool blankets inside and brought out a double-barrel shotgun. He opened the chamber and replaced the two shells inside with fresh ones. A half pint of whisky lay under the second blanket. He'd all but given up the drink a couple years after returning from the war against the states, but every so often he cheated.

The wind stopped. Floyd sat down on the bench and listened for a spell, then got up and entered Popcorn's stall, draped the wool blanket over the horse. Then he left the barn and half walked half trotted back to the house. The snow was deep— knee high, and it tugged at his pants cuffs as he went.

Kim tried shielding the candle as the door flew open. Floyd forced the door closed. He shook most of the snow off. "How's Popcorn?"

"Fine," Floyd said. "Hates the storm. Hates them all. Cain't say I blame 'em. Hate 'em too."

"You've been through worse than this ole storm."

In the closet he pulled out the Winchester rifle. He loaded it. Then he went to the window. He stared out at the barn.

"Limbs and trees are snappin' like matchsticks out there." He caught movement out of the corner of his eye. "You busy?"

"No. Why?"

"Blow the candle out. Thought I saw something move out there by the barn."

Kim blew the candle out, then joined her husband at the window. "We live on Black Mountain, dear. Could be anything. Snowstorms can play tricks." She snuggled up to the man she'd loved damn near her whole life. "What did you—"

"There it is again. Did you see it?"

"Could be—"

"What is it, Papa?"

"Jesus! There're two more."

Kim gripped Floyd's arm as she saw them cross the yard and said, "Hell are they?"

It did not take long for the night to turn white and everything to disappear. The trees slipped away as if they hadn't been there at all. The wind came and chased the snow all around, showing signs of life, then the wind calmed and the white powder reclaimed it again.

Kim and Floyd jumped as something hit the side of the cabin.

Whatever it was didn't take long to reach the roof.

And then it began to burrow its way in…

*

Below is a bit of dialog from my story *The Fight of the Century*. You'll find this in my collection *Strange Roads*.

Tom has been lured down into the world of underground fighting. They've promised him twenty-five thousand dollars if he beats the current champion. Some things aren't easily achieved, as Tom soon finds out.

The week went by without incident. In the underground locker room, Tommy sat on a table, feet dangling over a warped and badly cracked cement floor that'd seen better days. Lenny, a short pudgy man of about 72 walked into the room, a towel draped over one shoulder. His face puffy and red, his nose mashed nearly flat to his face. He walked with a slight hobble.

Lenny tossed the towel on the table next to Tommy. "Let's get those hands taped."

"Who am I fighting?"

"You'll see soon enough," Lenny said. "First the hands. Hold 'em out."

Tommy did. Lenny wrapped.

"Glad you showed," Lenny said. "Got a lot of money on this. So does the crowd out there. Way Edward tells it you got a helluva right hook. Said you took three guys at once down at Chick's last week. How are you feelin'?"

"Fine," Tommy said. "These locker rooms always smell like piss?"

"Yes. You will get used to it. We all do. Well, those of us who live down here. A lot of fighters have come and gone, kid. Some have even died in this very room. But not you. No, sir. You're gonna do us all a favor and cream this sumbitch." Lenny finished Tommy's right hand, and then moved over to the left. Tommy opened his hand palm down.

"I've never fought in a cage before," Tommy confessed.

"Feels odd."

His stomach began to knot up at the sound of the crowd in the arena.

"Never mind that. Fighting is fighting. You stay away from his blows, you hear? Do what you got to do, but don't let him land a punch."

"That powerful, huh?"

Lenny cringed as he finished taping Tommy's left hand. "Got nothin' to do with power, kid. Here, hold out your arms." Tommy did. Lenny ran his callused hands up Tommy's arms, massaging them. "Listen. You listening to me?"

"Yeah."

"You get to him first. Combinations. Jabs. Work on the body, break a few ribs soon as you can. But don't let him touch you. Careful with his arm bar. Seen'em break several arms with that one."

"How the hell am I supposed to do that? Run around the ring?"

"Just you listen." Lenny snatched up the towel he'd thrown on the table. He threw it across his shoulder. "Things are different down here in the underground, kid. Rules don't apply. Not with him. Not ever. Hear? You got sand. A whole damn lot. But there comes a time you got to have more than sand. This guy is mean."

"Who the hell am I fighting?"

"You'll find out soon enough."

The crowd roared, filling the catacombs of the underground as Tommy slid from the table. He danced and jigged and punched the air.

Lenny slipped the gloves on Tommy, said, "Don't you be getting all confident. He's fought twelve times. Six died right in this room."

"You can't be serious!"

"Yep. And things ain't been right since he come. Not right at all. Spectators thought it was neat having him here. Then things turned dark. Like I said, don't let him hit you. Not even once."

"I don't understand."

"Bad things happen when he hits his opponents."

"I'm sure it does. Broken nose. Ribs—"

"Stop laughing!"

"Be cool, Lenny. I got this."

"You got shit," Lenny said. "Others have said the same thing. They didn't. Listen. Every time he hits you, things come out of the dark. Nasty things. For instance, last time he fought a fellow named Jones. Jones damn near tore the guy's jaw right the hell off, but the guy recovered and came back with a massive uppercut. Bats came down out of the dark when that happened. God only knows where they came from. WHAM! And they were on him. Seconds later they ripped that poor bastard all to hell and back. Wasn't much left of' em. He died right here in this room. Right on this table."

*

In the early '90s, my older brother took a beating when he found his girlfriend in bed with another man. What ensued should have killed him. He lived to tell his story, thus opening a door years later for what you are about to read. Watch out for doors. Open them and make good use of what's inside. You never know…

Below is an excerpt called Johnny Be Good, which came to me a couple years ago. In the early '90s, my brother, John, touched death and lived to tell about it. The damage inflicted upon him should have sent him straight to the grave.

Johnny stepped out of the house dazed and confused and staggered to the sidewalk where he stood collecting his thoughts, or what thoughts floated by. After a while he hit the street, winding his way toward Eddie's Bar. He needed a drink.

As he walked, his head swam as if it'd been stove in with a jackhammer. Hangovers never impaired him, not even as a child sneaking whisky from his mother's cabinets. Never had he endured such riveting pain.

Johnny made it to the corner of Dent and Delmore and stopped to rest on a concrete wall and saw a boy about twelve approaching. He winced and mopped sweat out of his eyes. Everything swam around him as if in a dream. Real pain rained down on him, taking away the delirious notion it was a dream at all. He staggered as he sat, which he thought impossible. He wobbled side to side for a bit.

"Yo, Smooth?" The boy walked up. The man sat on a stretch of concrete wall. "You don't look so good."

"What is it, kid?" asked Johnny. "You following me?"

"Nope. You don't look so good. Your—"

"Why ain't you in school?"

"Ain't no school on Saturday."

"There should be."

"Can I have one of them?" The boy pointed to a smoldering cigarette between Johnny's fingers. "My daddy lets me smoke."

"He shouldn't."

"You gonna give me one or not?"

Johnny fished out one and laid it atop the concrete wall. "Your life, kid." He watched the kid with blurry eyes. If Johnny didn't know any better he'd think he'd been hit by a car instead of a bad hangover. The kid pulled out a book of matches and lit up. "Got a name, kid?"

"Jawan."

"Glad to meet ya," Johnny said. "They call me Johnny Be Good."

"Holy shit!"

"Watch it, kid."

"My daddy knows you. Said you killed a man in a bar once. Said you walked right up and broke his nose or somethin'."

"Jesus."

"It true? You really kill a man?"

Johnny couldn't remember if he had or not, to tell the truth. Surely he'd know this. Jesus, how fucked up was he? "If your daddy said so, I guess it's true." Johnny picked himself up on watery legs. His stomach lurched. "Go on, kid. Go find someone to play with."

With that Johnny walked on, staggering and fighting to keep his head up. The kid wasn't having any of that leaving stuff, so Johnny went on as if he didn't know he was there. People on the sidewalk crossed the street when they saw Johnny coming.

"Jesus, what's with people? Ain't they ever seen a man walking?"

"Tol' you, Smooth. You ain't lookin' so good."

"Why you following me?"

"You got smokes and I smoke them smokes, you let me."

"Go home, kid."

"You lost?"

"No."

"Where you goin'?"

"Eddie's bar."

"Ain't no Eddie's nowhere here, Smooth."

"Why you callin' me Smooth, kid?"

"I don't mean nuttin' by it. It's jus' how I talk. You know, like you white boys sayin' dude or somethin'," said the kid. "And you ain't even close to Eddie's. Eddie's is back that way."

Johnny said, "Shit," and sat down on a freshly cut lawn as cars passed by. He pulled out a cigarette and lit it. Then he lie back as he smoked. Wasn't long he got back on his feet and headed on, the boy following close behind.

Johnny walked for a long time and soon the sun dipped behind the lights of the city. "How far we come?" Johnny asked the boy. He knew the boy was there. "Kid?"

"How 'bout turning around, Smooth," said Jawan. "This ain't no good place."

"It's fine."

"It ain't fine, Smooth," said Jawan. "I don't even come down here. Kinda dark in this area, know what I mean? Crazy niggas run these streets after dark."

"I just gotta find Eddie's—"

"Toleja, Eddie's back where we come from."

Johnny stopped and looked at the kid. His vision blurred worse than ever as he mopped sweat out of his eyes. His clothes hung heavy with it. But the kid stood his ground. Johnny couldn't scare the kid off.

"Why you hangin' with me?" asked Johnny.

Jawan walked up close to Johnny. "'Cause you're all kinds of fucked up, Smooth." Jawan shook his head, walked ahead of Johnny. "We don't need to be down this way, man."

"It's all good, kid." Johnny said. "How long we been walkin'?"

"Too long."

"Goddamnit kid, how long?"

"About five miles."

"Time flies."

"Don't see how, you bein' messed up like you is," Jawan said. "Things 'bout to jam down here. Daytime is bad 'nough, but at night things get crazy. Please turn back, Smooth. I'll walk with ya back the other way. But not here."

Johnny looked back to see Jawan slowing. Was the look in the kid's eyes told Johnny the boy'd meant business.

"You stayin' or comin'?"

"Can't go no more with ya, Johnny," Jawan said. "You're on your own."

"Been on my own all my life, kid."

"You be careful. Stick to the alleys." Jawan watched as Johnny dug out his Winston cigarettes. He lit one and pulled on it and waved to the kid. Jawan waved back. Johnny went on as the streets and the darkness and sounds of the Chicago night swallowed him up.

Wasn't long before Johnny smelt burning wood and paper and saw cars, mostly Cadillacs, driving up and down the street. Abandoned homes overgrown with weeds stood gutted or partially burnt down like lost souls. The structures loomed above him as he staggered along the hardened streets.

And then a guitar riff cut through the night. The musician thrummed the chords to shut out the loud hum drum of the Chicago streets. Crying babies, gunfire, and a man shouting obscenities down the street were all gone. All but the riff. The riff went on, saturating the brick and mortar and wood of the buildings around him. The music moved Johnny in a way he couldn't quite explain. That unyielding melody masked everything. City noise faded. The wino on the sidewalk ahead and on the opposite side of Johnny walking away from him, seemed oblivious. Johnny wanted to shout at the old man to wake up and hear the music. But he didn't. He wanted it all to himself.

Johnny's pain eased the closer and louder the riff got.

A group of men clustered together ahead passed small bags

to each other, splitting up their take. Johnny ducked into an alley dotted with dumpsters and little lighting. He went on, staggering and fighting to stay on his feet. He came upon a mound of rags. The rags moved around a bit under a steam vent. Steam coiled and rose and disappeared into the night sky. Boots slipped out from under the rags. The bottoms of the boots had seen better days. The leather along the sides were peeled back like dried cow tongues, exposing flesh and soiled newspapers inside. A light winked out some good ways down the alley as Johnny went to walk on, but as he passed the bundle of rags, a head emerged. White eyes stared back at him. From behind he heard a click-clack sound he'd heard many years ago.

Balanced on an elbow, a man stared back at him. In his hand he held a sawed off double-barreled shotgun.

"Best be on your way," said the man with the sawed off.

"Calm it, Sam," said the other man. He rose up. Old rags he'd covered himself in trickled off him like paper. Johnny, even in his state, knew it gave little warmth to the man. Newspapers peeked out from under the sleeves and collar of his jacket, which wasn't much.

"Ain't calmin' nothin'," Sam said. "He was fixin' ta take our bottles."

"That true, mister? You fixin' to take our stuff?"

"No," Johnny said. "Passing through. Can you hear it? Tell me you hear the music."

"Man's ate up, Rodney."

"Hush it, Sam," Rodney said. "All's I hear is the crazies out there on the street. They don't come too much in the alleys. Safer in the alleys."

"Rodney!"

"I tol' you to hush it."

"I've been hearing it. It's all over the place."

"You following it?" Rodney got up and brushed the chill off. His bones popped as he straightened to his full height. He looked down at the man. Then he knelt and picked up his bottle. The ember-colored content swished around. He handed the bottle to Johnny, which Johnny drank greedily. "There you go. Drink it up. I've got another one."

"You gone nuts, Rodney?"

Johnny heard Sam get to his feet.

"Chill, Sam." Then to Johnny he said, "My little brother doesn't have the tolerance. But yeah, I heard it once. We got back from Nam, I followed it just like you is. That was back in '75."

"Two crazy mother-"

"Sam!"

"Fine, but he go ta gettin' rough, I'm puttin' him down."

"Fair 'nough," Rodney said. "Now shut it and let me talk." Rodney gathered himself and sat back down on the rags he used to cover up with. Cars drove up and down the dark streets. "Listen." He looked at Johnny. "Heard that riff back in the day. Don't rightly know what for, or who was there. All I know is you got to follow it. It's callin' you. Me, I cain't hear it no more. Maybe that's a good thing. But you...You got to go. Other than that riff, it ain't no safe place out here at night. And you're bleedin' to hell and back. Got your head busted, didn't ya?" Johnny put down his bottle, ran a hand across his head and almost screamed when it came away red. "See? Think I's liein'?"

"Shit."

"Shit's the least your problems."

*

Writing good dialog and building tension can take years. Pay close attention when people talk. And the best stories appear out of nowhere. Good ideas stick around. Your subconscious will delete the rest. And read those who write it best. This is the only way I know. There is no magic pixie dust to set atop our shoulders whispering secrets. Plain 'ole hard work will pay off. I promise. Writers who write effective dialog, some of the best are as follows: Ronald Kelly, Joe Lansdale, Charles Bukowski, Elmore Leonard, Earnest Hemingway, John Steinbeck, John Fante. Listen. I could give you a huge list of names, but you get the point.

Chapter Fourteen
Traditional Publishing vs Self-Publishing

It's a hard life, being a traditional writer. I won't lie. The worst part, you must travel it alone. Climbing to the top can be treacherous and unforgiving. Writers bleed much for what they want. It is a hunger not easily sated. You will witness the achievements and failures of others, so be happy for those who make it. Keep climbing because no one else will do it for you.

*

The road to self-publishing is as easy as it gets. The road is paved smooth and free of obstacles. All one has to do is go. But remember one thing, new writer, you'll never know if you're good enough if you start out this way. You'll never know the difference between a bad rejection letter or a great rejection letter. I'm going to give you some real life examples of rejections I've received.

Form rejection from a magazine:

Thank you for letting Three-lobed Burning Eye consider your story. Unfortunately, it didn't quite grab us. We wish you the best in finding its home.
Sincerely,
Andrew, Editor

I submitted *Strange Roads* to this agent. A great rejection:

Hi Steven, and thanks for thinking of me.
The sad reality is, getting a book of short stories published is difficult, and doubly so for an author without an extremely recognizable name. I like your writing, though, so if you have a novel/will have a novel soon, I'd love to take a look at that. But I just don't think I'd have any luck placing these stories, as fun as they are.
Of course, that's just my opinion, and another agent may very well feel differently. Thanks again for sending this my way, and talk soon.

Did you see that? I hooked a reputable agent. Self-publishing takes all the fun out of this. I want to know if I'm good enough. So should you. Submit traditionally first. Earn respect from your peers. Knowing you're good enough is a grand thing, guys. It's okay to be hard on yourself. Hone your skills, read daily and outside your genre.

Last year I wrote this quote and I live by it.

"I don't want to be one of those writers a publisher will publish just to make a buck. I want to be a writer a publisher wants to publish because I'm just that good."

Now if you're still hell-bent on self-publishing, then at least let me steer you in the right direction. Cover artists, editors and layout designers are key. Do it right the first time. Below is a list of book cover artists and interior layout designers and editors. These guys have been in the business a long time. Use them.

ZACH MCCAIN

Zach McCain is an internationally published artist who is primarily known for his illustration and cover artwork in the horror and science fiction genres. He has worked on hundreds of books for numerous publishers. His work ranges from book and magazine illustration to graphic design, album art, DVD and poster work for films, and RPG games. Mediums often used are oils as well as pencil, ink, and digital.

As a fan of Stephen King, Zach started out doing graphics and web work for The Dark Tower Compendium, a Stephen King fan website. He continued to do Stephen King fan artwork in his spare time and eventually got work with small horror publishers and Cemetery Dance Magazine. A couple of pieces of his fan artwork were featured in Knowing Darkness: The Art of Stephen King published by Centipede Press. He continues to do artwork for Stephen King projects, including books and film as well as private commissions for fans.

He is also the graphic designer for dark fiction publisher Dark-Fuse and he is currently working on his own comic book series in his spare time.

If you are a publisher, or an author looking to self-publish your book, and are in need of cover art and/or design work, feel free to contact Zach at:

zmccain@gmail.com | http://zachmccain.com/index.html

CÉSAR PUCH

Cesar is a wonderfully talented interior book designer. I've worked with Cesar many, many times. I've got nothing but the best from him. He'll work one-on-one with you when designing the text for your book. He can be contacted on Facebook:

https://www.facebook.com/cesar.puch

Owned and operated by award-winning author Kealan Patrick Burke, **ELDERLEMON DESIGN** provides affordable cover designs for authors. We cater to print and digital media, and each cover is made to order based on the author/client's own input. Employing stock art and our own photography, we work with you to ensure your finished cover accurately reflects your book's content in a dynamic, eye-catching way, and at the most competitive rates in the business.

Once you hire us to do your cover, we work with you to come up with a concept that's as close to what you want as you'll get without invasive surgery. After we schedule you, we offer a turnaround of not more than ten days from the assigned commencement date (excluding time incurred by additional changes requested by the author/client). To date we have designed covers for over seventy authors, including such notable names as Tim Lebbon, Brian Keene, Scott Nicholson, Richard Laymon, Bentley Little, Hugh Howey, J. Carson Black, and Vincent Zandri.

http://www.elderlemondesign.com/

GLENN CHADBOURNE is an American artist. He lives in Newcastle, Maine. He is best known for his work in the horror and fantasy genres, having created covers and illustrated books and magazines for publishers such as Cemetery Dance Publications, Subterranean Press, and Earthling Publications. Mr. Chadbourne is known for his sense of humor and down to earth manner, as well as the stark honesty of his work.

Glenn Chadbourne attended Lincoln Academy before continuing his education at The Portland School of Art. He also attended the University of Maine at Augusta, as well as the University of Southern Maine.

His first published work was in the late 1980s for the Stephen King related newsletter called Castle Rock. He won a contest that called for artists to submit something Stephen King related.

He wrote, illustrated, and self-published a few comics called ChillVille and Farmer Fiend's Horror Harvest in the early 1990s. He eventually met Rick Hautala and was asked to illustrate his short story collection Bedbugs. After Cemetery Dance Publications printed Bedbugs in 1999, things began to click for Mr. Chadbourne, and he has since illustrated work for many of the top names in the horror genre.

He recently illustrated The Secretary of Dreams: Volume 1, a graphic collection of Stephen King stories that was published by Cemetery Dance Publications in 2006 in three limited editions. Volume Two was announced as being drawn by Glenn Chadbourne in early 2007.

http://www.glennchadbourne.com/

ALAN MARSHALL CLARK is an author and an artist who is best known as the illustrator and book cover painter of many pieces of horror fiction. He was nominated for the Bram Stoker Award for Best First Novel for his 2005 book Siren Promised (co-written by Jeremy Robert Johnson).

He has won the World Fantasy Award for his illustrations ("Best Artist 1994"),[1] and he has won many Association of Science Fiction and Fantasy Artists' Chesley Awards. His book The Paint in My Blood was nominated for the "Best Art Book" for the 2005 Locus Awards. It was also nominated for the 2005 International Horror Guild Award for their "Non-fiction" category. His artwork has been featured on many signed limited editions from Cemetery Dance Publications, Lonely Road Books, Subterranean Press, Earthling Publications, and many other publishers of hardcovers as well as illustrations on the covers and interiors of textbooks, children's books, paperbacks, magazines and CDs.

He received his Bachelor of Fine Arts from the San Francisco Art Institute in 1979. He owns the publishing company, IFD Publishing (started in 1999). He currently lives in Eugene, Oregon with his wife Melody.

Mr. Clark is listed in the newest edition of Science Fiction and Fantasy Artists of the Twentieth Century: A Biographical Dictionary edited by Robert Weinberg, Jane Frank (McFarland & Company, 2009).

http://alanmclark.com/alanmclark.com/_Home_.html

KAREN BENNETT runs a proof reading site. She knows what she's doing. I've used her in the past:

https://www.facebook.com/Karen-Bennett-Freelance-Proofreader-749120908494520/?fref=ts

MICHAEL GARRETT is a brilliant editor. I've used him also. Michael is a bit pricy, but if you want Stephen King's first editor, you may want to check him out. He does an in-depth edit of your book. He charges upfront. Trust me. He's good.

http://www.manuscriptcritique.com

Chapter Fifteen

Books and Videos
Every Aspiring Writer
Should Read/Watch

Stephen King: *On Writing. A Memoir of the Craft.*

Starve Better: *Surviving the Endless Horror of the Writing Life* by Nick Mamatas. This is a must for any aspiring writer!

Elmore Leonard's *10 Rules of Writing Writers on Writing Vol.3: An Author's Guide* (Writers On Writing: An Author's Guide: Crystal Lake Publishing.)

Charles Bukowski Documentary

I love how Ian McEwan talks about the writing life. You can watch this on YouTube.

John Irving gives us his thoughts on publishing, and advice to aspiring writers.

https://www.youtube.com/watch?v=QHfWv1QAzE8

Elmore Leonard on Writing

https://www.youtube.com/watch?v=PeZQl2nvnfM

I'm going to leave you with a quote from one of the finest writers of the 20th Century. It rang true then, it still rings true today.

If what a writer wrote was published and sold many, many copies, the writer thought he was great. If what a writer wrote was published and sold a medium number of copies, the writer thought he was great. If what a writer wrote was published and sold very few copies, the writer thought he was great. If what the writer wrote never was published and he didn't have the money to publish it himself, then he thought he was truly great. The truth, however, was that there was very little greatness. It was almost nonexistent, invisible. But you could be sure that the worst writer had the most confidence, the least self-doubt.

—Charles Bukowski

I hope you walk away with a little more knowledge about the writing biz than you knew. As I said above, take everything I've said with a grain of salt.

The Wooden Box put me on the literary map a few years ago. I hope you enjoy it as much as I enjoyed writing it.

The Wooden Box

The Wooden Box

Mack Grainy didn't notice the sun going down. He'd been working in the barn, chiseling away at the smooth pine box ever since Nora took sick six months ago. As he stood up to stretch his legs, he heard a flutter of wings.

About a year ago an owl made its residence in the rafters. At night, if you took a mind to, you could stay up and watch it come and go from the barn to the meadow searching for rats. Most times, though, it just hooted a lot. Kind of raised the hair on the back of your neck if you've never heard one before.

The barn itself, a towering structure of aged cedar and oak consisted of a loft and four central stalls, all of which stood empty except the one on the end. That was Minny's. Minny was their last and only livestock, a kicking rough neck of a mule that'd plant your face to the other side if she didn't know you. Mack wanted to eliminate the stall gate at one time or another, but Minny kicked the damn thing off its rusting hinges one night. Guess she liked it that way. She'd go out and graze in the morning, trot back in the afternoon. They let her have the run of the barn.

Mack finished for the day, threw a tarp over the box, then went to the house.

Inside he sat at the kitchen table, rolled up a badly wrinkled newspaper. He swatted an assemblage of flies perched on the table. He missed all but three. "Damn things," he said. They scuttled up the walls and kitchen counters. He knew why they were here. Nora. They were waiting for her to die. He wanted things to be normal again, like they used to be. But that wasn't going to happen. He faced the facts a long time ago. She was dying and there was nothing to be done about it. He smacked the table again scattering the winged bandits into the air. No matter how much tape he hung from the ceiling, they kept coming.

Cancer stole Nora's leg this past winter. Toenails rotted away, and then her foot went all grayish-black. She'd lost it from the knee down. That was that. She lost her will right then and there. Due to the fact that the doctors hadn't overlapped enough tissue to smooth out the stump, the bone jutted out like an ivory colored fence post that'd been gnawed on. The cancer spread so fast there was nothing else could be done. They gave her six months to a year.

He left the table, filled a pot with water. He placed it on the cook stove to warm. Even in the summer, when the heat came on without mercy, and before the illness stole her, she loved a warm bath. He collected two rags, one for drying, the other for washing, placed them over one wide shoulder, and walked into the bedroom.

Nora was lying beneath four quilts. Her eyes were closed. By the time he'd placed the pot on the nightstand and sat down, she opened her eyes. "Thought you gone and forgot me," she said.

"Never," Mack said as he soaked a rag, lathered it up with soap. "Been busy is all."

"Cain't cook. Cain't even get outta bed no more," she said. "Done with my box?"

"Why you in such a hurry to die, Nora? I want you around for a bit."

She'd been a hell of a cook in her day. When they had the chili cook-off, four counties converged on the small town of Goreville. Nora won each year.

Then there were the four travelers last year. Said they came from East Texas. Mack'd seen his fair share of rag-tags, but these four had had it bad. They'd looked like they'd been chewed up and spit out. Life had done this. No mercy for those on the road. They'd asked about work. Mack told them no work needed done, so Nora invited them to bed down in the barn and a meal. She'd cooked up a mess of white beans, cornbread, and mashed tatters. The next morning they were gone. Mack had gone out to the barn to fetch them for breakfast, but they'd skipped out sometime before dawn. Mack tore away from the thoughts when he heard Nora.

"Macky," she said softly. "When's it gonna be time?"

Only two women called him that, and one of' em been gone morin' thirty years. Man called him that he'd split their skull with a fist or axe handle. "Don't you worry none," Mack said. "You get your rest. I'll deal with all that." Looking around the room, he took in the wallpaper. Flowers. God, how she loved the damn things.

Once Nora called from the house for Mack to de-weed the flowers around the house. Though she loved her flowers, Nora hated de-weeding them. Whatever caused her to think he liked doing it was beyond him. Had it been his way, they'd never been planted.

An hour later he'd stepped into the house for a jar of water and to sit a spell. He noticed her sitting at the table and thought he'd best get on out to the barn. Make himself busy, case she wanted the house painted.

Mack was almost to the door when she asked, "You de-weed them plants?"

"Course," he'd said. "That's what I been doin' since you told me to. Why? Got something else for me to do?" He answered too quickly, God knows, and she got up, pushed the chair under the table. He *had* de-weeded them, not just in the way she would've liked. Truth to tell, he'd pulled up every last one of' em. In that moment he'd wished those damn flowers would've sprouted back up in a hurry, 'cause Nora had gone all stiff like. Her eyes narrowed.

"Did, huh," she'd said, easing herself toward the door. "Do a good job?"

Mack put his hand on the brass door knob, hoping to keep her inside a while longer. And when she'd reached the door he'd felt a single line of sweat drip off the end of his nose. "Good as I could, yes," Mack said. "What you doin'?" he asked, blocking the door a little more. "Too dang hot out there. I took care of it. No need goin' out there."

Her eyes'd gone all wild then, and she'd leapt on him like a rabid bobcat, hitting and slapping. Mack took the punches, and managed to open the door and stumble outside onto the porch. By then she'd crawled from his front to his back and was pounding something awful when she saw the yard brightly lit in different colors. He'd felt a few of them punches. Mack found her swinging arm and pulled hard, throwing her off of him and into the yard. She'd hit the ground so hard dust kicked up all around her. He got scared and ran to her. He picked her up and dusted her off, asked if she was all right. She was. A moment later they were in stitches and fixing to bust.

"Meanest man in four counties, huh," she'd said laughing. "Cain't wait till the girls in town hear this."

Mack was doubled over laughing. "Better not," he'd said between fits of laughter. But his laugher was short lived as Nora took to her feet, crossed her arms against her chest.

"You plant them flowers back this spring, Macky Grainy," Nora had said. "Or I'll spill the beans, and our bed will be a little less filled. You hear?"

So Mack agreed and replanted those infernal things the following spring. Plus Nora kept her promise, which he was grateful for.

Six months later the depression hit. Two years after that the cancer found Nora.

*

Now he was cleaning and washing bed sores. Some oozed greenish puss, while others were quarter size and gaping. He poured peroxide in the deep ones. She screamed and swatted and cussed 'til the pain ebbed and she was out of breath. Mack never faulted her for it.

Finished, he placed the rags in the pot. He disappeared into the other room. He came back with her wheelchair. He put her in that, and then stripped the bedding. Mack collected fresh linen from a chest of drawers, made the bed. Then he laid her on the bed again and covered her. Mack was turning to leave when she asked the question she kept asking since the cancer took over.

"You gone do it soon, Macky?" she asked. "Can you still do it?"

Mack stood at the door with his back to her. He had nothing. Words escaped him. And then he finally said, "I can." Tears welled up in his eyes. "I can do it."

"When?"

"Soon," Mack said. "Soon."

"How soon, Macky?" she asked. "Cause the pains startin' to come more now. I can't live like this."

"I know," said Mack. His hands trembled so badly the pot of water threatened to slip from his grasp. He turned to face her. "A few days. All right? I promise."

Nora said nothing more and closed her eyes. Soon he heard the rhythm of her breathing and left the room. He put the pot in the sink. He found the good book in an old china cabinet. Its cover was black leather and tattered, the pages torn from handling and age. The words *Holy Bible* had virtually faded away. Mack ran his strong, liver-spotted hand along its aged exterior. Nora had read the book cover to cover over the years to the point the bindings had split and frayed.

He should've bought her a new one. Mack had never been the religious type. All the things he'd done in his youth and later in the war, he expected his hands to catch fire when he touched its cover, but they didn't. He opened the book, fumbled clumsily through the blasted thing until he found the verse she wanted inscribed on the box. He read the verse for the first time and cried.

*

The next morning Nora and Mack ate breakfast in silence. Their eyes met a few times, but no words were exchanged. After they finished Mack was collecting their plates, when Nora touched his wrist and stared up into his dark brown eyes.

"Today?" asked Nora. "Is it today?"

"Not today," Mack said. "Got the inscription to finish. But soon."

"Wish we could dance like we once did," Nora said. "Sure could use some of that. 'member?"

"I do," Mack said swallowing back tears. "You could really kick up them heels."

On Friday nights Mack and Nora used to turn on the music box and tear up the living room dancing. They drank from the jug, and before the night ended they were tripping over one another, tangled together so badly a pry bar could not have peeled them apart.

They made funny in bed until the sun bled through the trees. When they'd finally pulled themselves out of bed in the afternoon their heads pounded and bones ached.

Mack left the room and cleaned the plates. When he looked in on her again he saw she'd fallen asleep. This might not be as bad as the doctors warned, Mack thought. Might be all she'd get. He could deal with this, even though she was still asking him to do it. Perhaps she'd just slip away peacefully in her sleep.

He was wrong.

*

The next week Nora's pain burrowed in deep as if it had claws and a mind of its own, made its home in her bones. Her flesh took on a yellowish-green hue. She was near skeletal now at eighty-five pounds. Her once vibrant eyes were sunk back within their sockets, and her movements were limited.

Mack split his day between the barn and caring for Nora. He sat down next to the wooden box, pulled on a jug of lightening old man Peters dropped off few days ago. Old man Peters was their local postman. They shared many a drink together over the years.

Then he went back to work, cutting out the words Nora wanted, all under the watchful eye of Minny. Once she sauntered over and nudged him with her head, something she never did. Mack expected to get a mouth full of horseshoe, but that didn't happen.

After a while his hands got to hurting so he got up and swept out Minny's stall and filled her water. He brought her in some fresh hay. It gave him time to think of something other than that damn old box, which to be honest, he was proud of. He knew Nora would love it and that's all that mattered.

Finished with Minny, Mack swept out the entire barn. At the work bench, he gathered up what tools he wasn't using, put them away. They were scattered to hell and back. It needed to be done. Mack came upon his old trench mace. A short wooden handled club with a steel ball and jutting spikes on the business end. He'd used it a few times after taking it from a German officer in a trench. Made a real mess of a fella if you used it right. A few Germans lost their jaws, teeth and gums under its weight.

And without warning it hit him full in the chest, his body, his mind, and his soul. It bathed over him so strongly he couldn't keep it down any longer. Mack Grainy cried long and hard.

Minny snorted, tapped the earthen floor playfully as if she understood. She walked over to Mack and nudged him again.

It was time.

Mack found Nora awake. The screaming passed an hour ago. The doctors gave them morphine for when the pain settled in. It came in real handy. She was alert, as if she knew by the look on his face. But before she could ask, Mack said, "In the morning. No sooner. I want us to watch the sunrise together," he said as he watched her face beam. It was almost as if she were young again. That vibrant, colorful girl he'd met just after the war. She'd hate him for leaving the farm once she was gone, but he felt it better not to tell her. No need making her last few hours heart-wrenching. No need stayin' around here without her. It'd just bring back long-lost memories he wouldn't be able to bear.

Mack sat next to her on the bed for a long time. He held her frail, cold hand for the last time.

*

In the morning before dawn, Mack wheeled in the chair, woke her. Her eyes fluttered open, confused for a moment and then remembered. "Ready?" Mack asked.

"Been ready," she said. "You?"

"No," Mack said. "Rather Minny kick me in the teeth than do this."

"It'll be over soon."

Mack said, "Want you to see the box first. Figure it took me six month to build it, least you could do is see it."

In the barn, Nora ran her hands along the smooth, wooden box. The varnish gleamed under the oil lamp's amber light. It hung by a nail in a beam next to the box. "Guess this is where all the coffee went, huh?"

"Makes for good varnish," Mack said. "Besides, you quit drinking coffee years ago." He ran his hand through her thinning gray hair. It was long, flowing and soft. She'd made sure to have him wash it everyday. It was the only thing on her that didn't carry the scent of death.

"Pick me up," she said. "I want to read the inscription." He did. She ran her hands along the verse. She read it aloud as if it were her final attempt to save his soul. Mack didn't have the heart to stop her.

"The Lord is my Shepherd; I shall not want. He maketh me to lie down in green pastures: He leadeth me beside the still waters." She stopped and looked back at him. "We have time?"

"We got time," Mack said. "You been goin' through the shadow of death all these months. You've earned the right to finish it."

"He restoreth my soul: He leadeth me in the paths of righteousness for His name's sake. Yea, though I walk through the valley of the shadow of death, I will fear no evil: For thou art with me; Thy rod and thy staff, they comfort me. Thou preparest a table before me in the presence of mine enemies; Thou annointest my head with oil; My cup runneth over. Surely goodness and mercy shall follow me all the days of my life, and I will dwell in the House of the Lord forever." She looked up into those big brown eyes of his. Held onto him the best she could.

"You done real good, Macky. So good." She saw Minny then. A make-shift trailer was hitched to her. The trailer was at an angle low enough to slide the box up onto. Minny stared back at her. She didn't move. She almost looked frightening in the light's amber glow. "Now," Nora said. "Let's get to that sunrise."

*

Mack wheeled her to the back of the house for the event. He thought about things as they went. He thought about the farm and what would happen to it once he was gone. Surprisingly enough, he wondered if Nora's God would greet him as a friend when it was his time or would Nora be there to greet him at a place she said was the pearly gates. If all that was true would he walk with her on streets of gold?

They were at the back of the house when the light seeped through the trees. The early dawn sky turned a bloodshot red, and soon the sky shifted in brighter colors.

Mack stood next to his wife of fifty years, hand on her shoulder. They did not speak. No pain could've been bad enough to tear this moment away from them. For now she was at peace. For now the pain could not touch her. When the sun was even with the tree tops, Mack leaned down, kissed her cheek gently and stepped back.

He fished his revolver out of his pocket and put one round in the back of her head. The impact nearly sent her out of the wheelchair.

Mack stood there long after the sun had risen. He cried so hard he thought he might have broken some ribs, or at least fractured some. Long after the cool morning air turned hot and sticky and breathtaking, Mack wheeled her to the barn, laid her in the box and nailed the lid down, all under the watchful eye of Minny. He tapped Minny's ass gently, guiding her out back of the barn.

A few months ago he dug up a place for Nora with the tractor. Mack backed Minny up toward the hole and when she was where he needed her, he slid the box off the trailer. He unhitched Minny, leaving her without the burden of the trailer. She ambled back to the barn.

Mack sat next to the box, and as Nora had done, he ran his hand along the box. "You're at peace now, ol' girl," he said. There wasn't much left to do. His breath caught in his throat as he put the revolver under his chin and pulled the trigger.

*

A week later, Brian Peters found the hole, the box and Mack when he delivered the post. Not soon after that, he discovered Minny gave up the ghost, too. She lay on the stall floor stiff as a board. Flies got to her pretty bad. The whole barn smelt of her. Guess she figured with the two gone, she had nothing left to give.

Brian drove back into town forgetting about delivering the mail for the day, and got help. They finished what Mack started. They buried all three bodies properly.

*

Three weeks later, Brian Peters was driving past the old Grainy farm and saw something that caused his chest to hitch. A single light burned in the farm's window, and inside he saw two people kicking up their heels dancing as if they were having the time of their lives.

STEVEN LLOYD writes out of Southern Illinois, and has interviewed such authors and actors as Jack Ketchum, Nancy Collins, legendary film greats Bill Moseley and Sid Haig, from the "Devil's Rejects" films. His work has appeared in numerous print and on-line publications. In 2008 Lloyd launched a publishing company called Croatoan Publishing, dedicated to the Horror and Dark Suspense genre. Before closing the doors, Lloyd released "People are Strange" by James Newman and "Flesh Welder" by Ronald Kelly. In 2014 his collection Strange Roads was recommended for the Bram Stoker Award. You can contact him here: steven_28652@msn.com

MARK SIEBER has been reading and watching horror, science fiction, and other things for five decades. He is the owner and operator of horrordrive-in.com, and is the editor of Horror Drive-In Presents An Old Night Short Story Marathon. Mark's columns, predictable titled Horror Drive-In, are featured in Cemetery Dance Magazine and Cemetery Dance Online. He knows good horror fiction when he reads it.

RONALD KELLY has been writing his unique brand of Southern-fried horror for nearly thirty years. His work includes such novels as Undertaker's Moon, Blood Kin, Burnt Magnolia, Fear, and Hell Hollow, as well short story collections like Cumberland Furnace, Midnight Grinding, The Sick Stuff, and After the Burn. He lives in a backwoods hollow in Brush Creek, Tennessee with his wife and three young'uns.

www.ingramcontent.com/pod-product-compliance
Lightning Source LLC
Chambersburg PA
CBHW032031290526
45786CB00011B/1374